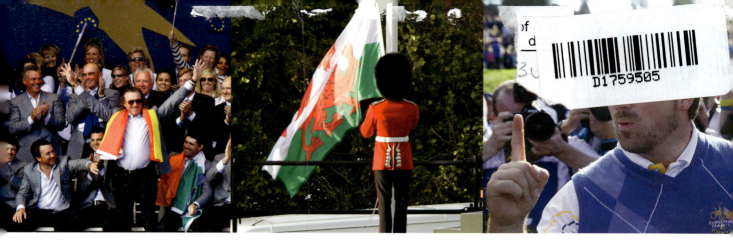

My Ryder Cup
The longest weekend
by David Williams

The Ryder Cup is special. It has a record of inspiring players to the peaks of their abilities, to create some of the greatest moments in golf. Equally, it has often proved to be an emotional rollercoaster for players and spectators alike. But the 2010 contest was unlike any other; producing drama, tension and exhilaration across four days of thrilling competition.

Photography photolibrarywales.com

GRAFFEG

Published by Graffeg
Copyright © Graffeg 2010
ISBN 978 1 905582 57 0

Graffeg, Radnor Court,
256 Cowbridge Road East,
Cardiff CF5 1GZ Wales, UK
T: +44 (0)29 2078 5156
sales@graffeg.com
www.graffeg.com

My Ryder Cup, the longest
weekend. Words and pictures
© copyright David Williams 2010.

Designed and produced by
Peter Gill & Associates
sales@petergill.com
www.petergill.com

Graffeg are hereby identified
as the Authors of this work in
accordance with Section 77 of the
Copyrights, Designs and Patents
Act 1988.

UK distribution:
Gardners Books
www.gardners.com
sales@gardners.com

Welsh Books Council
www.cllc.org.uk
castellbrychan@cllc.org.uk

A CIP catalogue record for this
book is available from the
British Library

Our thanks to Mitchell Platts,
PGA European Tour for his advice
and support.

Every effort has been made to
ensure that the information given
in this book is current and it is
given in good faith at the time of
publication.

Graffeg books are available from
all good bookshops and online
from www.graffeg.com

Photography by David Williams
and Andrew Orchard, with
additional material from
David Angel p8, 9, Phil Rees p4
and Paul Mattock p11, 16, 17, 20,
21, 22, 23, 173.

Contents

The Celtic Manor Resort

'£40 million isn't too much to spend on a round of golf!' Sir Terry Matthews

For Sir Terry Matthews, owner of The Celtic Manor Resort, the first weekend of October 2010 was the culmination of a long personal journey. He was born in the Lydia Beynon Maternity Hospital, at the base of the hill on which his five-star resort hotel now stands. A natural entrepreneur, he has remained true to his roots while building highly successful telecommunications and networking businesses in Wales and Canada.

In 1980, Sir Terry bought the old hospital, which he had noticed was boarded up, and turned it into a seventy-bedroom hotel, which remains part of the resort. He then began a programme of development and expansion which, some thirty years later, has seen the site grow into a luxurious leisure resort, spa and conference centre.

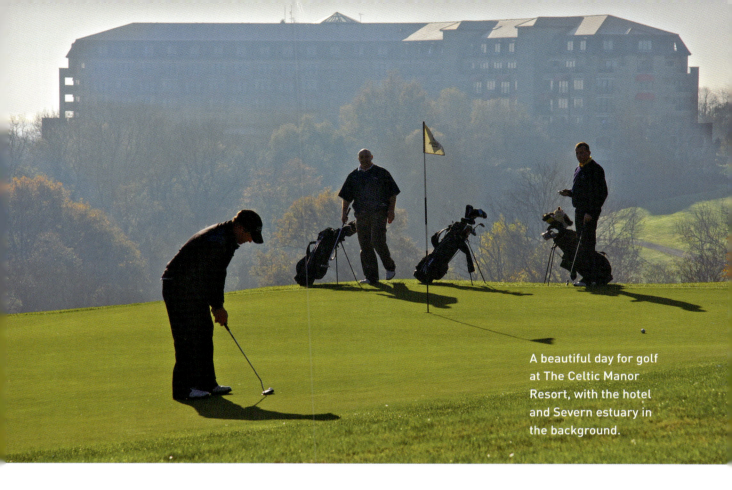

A beautiful day for golf at The Celtic Manor Resort, with the hotel and Severn estuary in the background.

Set in 1400 acres of landscaped parkland, it has three golf courses: The Roman Road, The Montgomerie and The Twenty Ten Course, on which The Ryder Cup 2010 was played. The Golf Academy, which opened in 1995, provides professional tuition at all levels. It is a centre of excellence for the Golf Union of Wales, offering driving ranges, practice greens, a shop, equipment hire and the option of video analysis of your swing.

Sir Terry's original vision was certainly not based merely on the sentiment of a local boy. He realised that the strategically positioned site, at the southern gateway to Wales and just a couple of hours west of London and Heathrow Airport along the M4 motorway, had tremendous potential. His investment of £140 million in developing the resort was the largest private

investment in the UK hospitality industry. His judgement proved correct and the resort has since been hailed a great success, earning many awards for its accommodation, conference centre, restaurants and golf courses.

The ultimate accolade came in 2001 when, with the support of the Welsh Assembly Government, and in hot competition with other venues, The Celtic Manor Resort was chosen to host the 2010 Ryder Cup. The world's most prestigious golf tournament – and the world's third-largest sporting event in terms of global media coverage after the Olympic Games and the soccer World Cup – would be visiting Wales for the first time.

This was the signal to do something completely new, namely to design a golf course specifically for The Ryder Cup. The result – The Twenty Ten Course – involved a further investment of

The Celtic Manor Resort

The Twenty Ten Clubhouse and the eighteenth green.

£40 million. It extends along the scenic valley and provides many satisfying challenges, including spectacular water hazards on half its holes. In recent years, the Wales Open competitions provided opportunities to refine the design of the course and to enable the The Celtic Manor Resort to become adept at accommodating large and enthusiastic crowds.

The early holes have the feel of a links course; long rough, deep bunkers and tricky swales. The water hazards make their presence felt in the middle section. From the fifteenth onwards, it becomes a matter of adapting to varying gradients on the hillside and, early and late in the year, playing towards the setting sun.

The fourteenth, considered the toughest hole on the course, calls for a confident drive and a bold second shot, avoiding the lake. The fifteenth can be tackled by a drive past the trees that almost obscure it, but stray left and you discover either a picturesque creek or a deep bunker from which the pin is invisible. The eighteenth, in its natural amphitheatre, provides a perfect conclusion either to a major competition or to a round with friends.

The Twenty Ten Clubhouse opened in 2007. It features the airy, cedar-beamed Rafters Restaurant (warmed by a crackling log fire); a members' lounge with leather Chesterfield armchairs and an open hearth; luxurious oak-panelled locker rooms and (as the 'nineteenth hole') a pleasant spike bar where members and guests may relax after their round. The long balcony offers wide views over the eighteenth hole and fairway to the rest of the course and along the Usk valley.

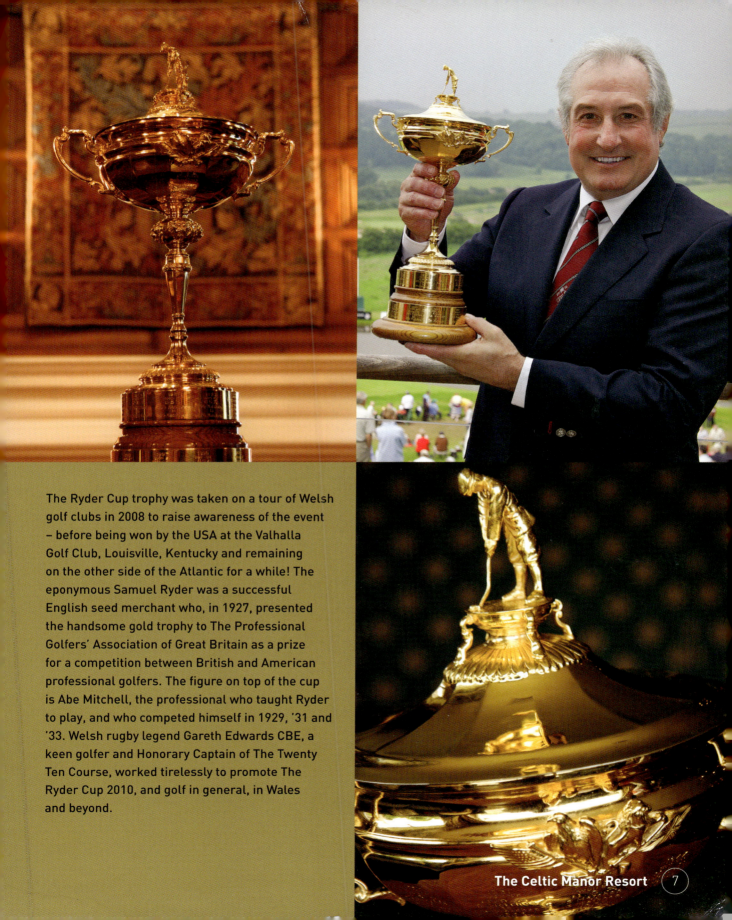

The Ryder Cup trophy was taken on a tour of Welsh golf clubs in 2008 to raise awareness of the event – before being won by the USA at the Valhalla Golf Club, Louisville, Kentucky and remaining on the other side of the Atlantic for a while! The eponymous Samuel Ryder was a successful English seed merchant who, in 1927, presented the handsome gold trophy to The Professional Golfers' Association of Great Britain as a prize for a competition between British and American professional golfers. The figure on top of the cup is Abe Mitchell, the professional who taught Ryder to play, and who competed himself in 1929, '31 and '33. Welsh rugby legend Gareth Edwards CBE, a keen golfer and Honorary Captain of The Twenty Ten Course, worked tirelessly to promote The Ryder Cup 2010, and golf in general, in Wales and beyond.

Twenty Ten course

With the river Usk meandering by, the Twenty Ten Course is both spectacularly located and easily accessible. The extent of the water hazards, with some presenting the dilemma of whether to go over or around them, is evident. The variety of the terrain – from the banks of the river to the hillside character (and views) of the later holes – makes this an especially pleasing course to play. The entrance to The Celtic Manor Resort and its three golf courses is close to Junction 24 on the M4 motorway at Newport.

Hole	Par	Yards	Hole	Par	Yards
1	4	465	10	3	210
2	5	610	11	5	562
3	3	189	12	4	458
4	4	461	13	3	189
5	4	433	14	4	485
6	4	422	15	4	377
7	3	213	16	4	499
8	4	439	17	3	211
9	5	580	18	5	575
Out	36	3,812	In	35	3,566
			Total	71	7,378

River Usk

'We wanted to create a fantastic stage for the players to walk down.'
Ross McMurray, Course designer

Practice days

The scene was set. Twenty-four of the world's best golfers arrived at The Celtic Manor Resort, their home for the next week.

Europe's top players, under the captaincy of Colin Montgomerie, made their way independently, some directly from other competitions. The USA team, led by Corey Pavin, flew into Cardiff airport – bringing with them The Ryder Cup.

'We are very pleased to be here. The welcome here in Wales is fantastic. We are looking forward to a good week, a great competition, great sportsmanship out there.'
USA Captain Corey Pavin

Years of careful preparation had brought The Twenty Ten Course to a peak of verdant perfection. Surely no golf course had ever received more care – more skilful cutting, dressing, rolling, feeding and tender loving care – at the hands of more dedicated groundsmen.

The permanent staff of The Celtic Manor Resort was joined by an army of volunteer marshalls, additional groundsmen and an enormous supporting cast including caterers, shop assistants, police, paramedics, security personnel, car-park attendants and park-and-ride bus drivers. More than 7,000 people knew exactly what their responsibilities would be once the event got under way.

Gwent Police rehearsed meticulous plans for handling the safe and smooth management of up to 50,000 spectators each day. A temporary bus station was made ready to receive the multitude. A fleet of 100 BMW cars would ferry players, officials and VIPs wherever they wished to go. Representatives of the world's media, including every major golfing magazine, formed and wrote their first impressions. Messages of goodwill were received from Her Majesty Queen Elizabeth II; President Barack Obama; José Manuel Barroso, President of the European Commission; and The Right Honourable Carwyn Jones AM, First Minister of Wales.

At the centre of everything, the captains, vice-captains and players settled in and looked forward to several days of practice and familiarisation with the Twenty Ten Course, which many of them were seeing for the first time.

'This is the first time I've arrived with no golf clubs, I assure you. Strange in many ways – biggest event in my golfing career and I've come here with no clubs. Quite weird really.'
European Captain Colin Montgomerie OBE

'The golf course has had rave reviews from all twelve players. Fantastic, the work that Jim McKenzie and his staff have done in preparation here.'

Colin Montgomerie

'The rough is thick. It's hard to get out of, but the fairways are the same widths as they were for the Wales Open when I played a year-and-a-half ago. It's set up very fairly. It's going to reward good play.'

Corey Pavin

BER 2010   THE CELT

'It's just so neat to be a part of a team; we don't get to do it very often.'

Tiger Woods

OME TO THE 2010 RYDER CUP

RYDER CUP
1927 — 2010
CELTIC MANOR

OFFICIAL PARTNERS OF
THE 2010 RYDER CUP

BMW
citi
Emirates
KPMG
ROLEX

Even the practice days attracted large crowds – upwards of 15,000 dedicated golf fans, their vocal enthusiasm hinting at the role the spectators would play in the competition itself.

'When you get here, you realise the importance of it and you realise how big it is and how important it is to everyone; I don't want to let myself down this week and I don't want to let anyone else down – and that's the big thing.'
Rory McIlroy

Ian Poulter and Graeme McDowell enjoy the relaxed camaraderie that makes The Ryder Cup such a special experience for the players.

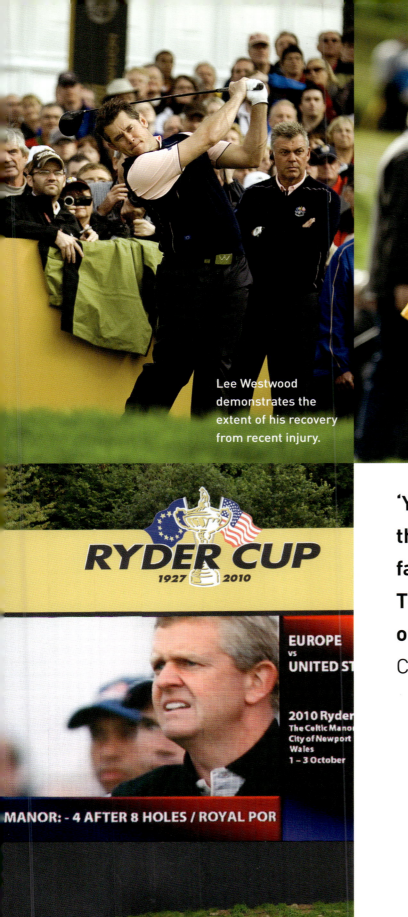

Lee Westwood demonstrates the extent of his recovery from recent injury.

RYDER CUP
1927 2010

EUROPE
vs
UNITED ST

2010 Ryder
The Celtic Manor
City of Newport
Wales
1 – 3 October

MANOR: - 4 AFTER 8 HOLES / ROYAL POR

'Yes, on paper, it's been said that we – Europe – are the favourites. Unfortunately, The Ryder Cup is not played on paper.'

Colin Montgomerie

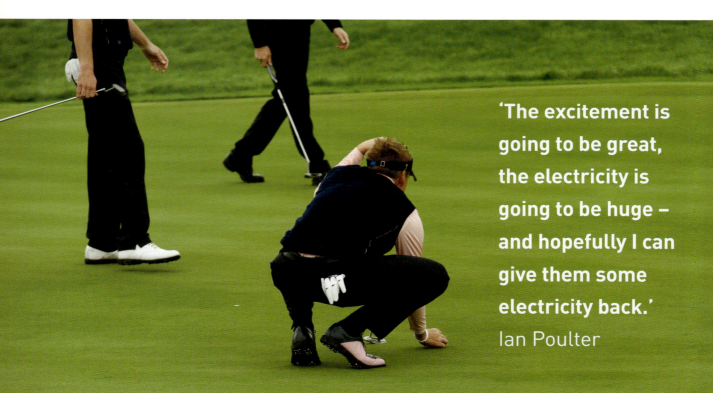

'The excitement is going to be great, the electricity is going to be huge – and hopefully I can give them some electricity back.'

Ian Poulter

Players, caddies and spectators get to know the course in the generally fair weather of the practice days.

As the final practice sessions drew to a close, having attracted substantial crowds, both teams reported their satisfaction with the course and looked forward to the start of competition.

Opening ceremony

Thursday afternoon arrived and the practice sessions ended. A large crowd gathered for the opening ceremony, during which the teams would be introduced by their captains and, this being Wales, could count on being welcomed by some excellent music!

Two blocks of empty seats on the large stage began to fill as team officials, wives and partners, and representatives of golf's upper echelons were introduced. The loudest cheers – and they were very loud indeed – were reserved for the team members themselves as they walked, heads held high, through the crowd to their places.

Sir Terry Matthews sat with the European team, evidently moved by the realisation that his great dream was about to become reality. Gareth Edwards was there too, his role as Honorary Captain of The Twenty Ten Course adding a new dimension to his distinguished career as an international sportsman.

Carwyn Jones, First Minister of Wales, welcomed everyone warmly and described the attractions of this small but outstandingly beautiful nation – including its suitability as a place in which to invest and do business. He praised Sir Terry Matthews for his imagination and tenacity in bringing The Ryder Cup to Wales and commended the staff of The Celtic Manor Resort for their thorough preparations.

Jim Remy, President of the PGA of America, and Phil Weaver of the PGA of Great Britain and Ireland, spoke of the significance of The Ryder Cup. They emphasised its traditions of fair play and sportsmanship, founded on Samuel Ryder's vision of a contest played for honour rather than for any monetary prize.

José Manuel Barroso, President of the European Commission, pointed out that this is the one event in which Europe is represented by a single team, and spoke highly of the Welsh welcome. Sir Terry Matthews beamed contentedly throughout!

'When you're standing up there and you are announced by one of the top players in Europe to be part of The Ryder Cup, that was a very proud moment for me.'
Martin Kaymer

Welsh Guards raise the flags of the United States, the European Union and the participating European nations.

The mezzo-soprano
Katherine Jenkins
delights the audience.

'This great sporting event places Wales firmly on the map as one of the world's top golfing destinations.'

Carwyn Jones,
First Minister of Wales

My Ryder Cup The longest weekend

Stewart Cink, below, is eventually introduced, much to the amusement of Tiger Woods and team mates.

'**Yeah, I only forgot one player – it could have been two, could have been worse. I'm very excited that the matches are about to start. I can't wait to watch them, just like you!'**
Corey Pavin, USA Captain, on having forgotten to introduce one of his players, Stewart Cink, during the opening ceremony.

Teams

Europe

Lee Westwood, England

Ian Poulter, England

Edoardo Molinari, Italy

Francesco Molinari, Italy

Rory McIlroy, N. Ireland

Graeme McDowell, N. Ireland

Martin Kaymer, Germany

Miguel Ángel Jiménez, Spain

Pádraig Harrington, N. Ireland

Peter Hanson, Sweden

Ross Fisher, England

Luke Donald, England

Captain

Colin Montgomerie, Scotland

Vice Captains

Thomas Bjørn, Darren Clarke, Sergio Garcia and Paul McGinley, augmented by José María Olazábal

USA

Phil Mickelson, California

Hunter Mahan, California

Bubba Watson, Florida

Jim Furyk, Pennsylvania

Steve Stricker, Wisconsin

Dustin Johnson, South Carolina

Jeff Overton, Indiana

Matt Kuchar, Florida

Zach Johnson, Iowa

Tiger Woods, California

Stewart Cink, Alabama

Rickie Fowler, California

Captain

Corey Pavin, California

Vice Captains

Paul Goydos, Tom Lehman,
Davis Love III and Jeff Sluman

Day 1
Friday 1st October
Fourballs

USA		Europe	Score
Phil Mickelson / Dustin Johnson	Lost to	Lee Westwood / Martin Kaymer	3 & 2
Stewart Cink / Matt Kuchar	Halved	Rory McIlroy / Graeme McDowell	Halved
Tiger Woods / Steve Stricker	Defeated	Ross Fisher / Ian Poulter	2 Up
Bubba Watson / Jeff Overton	Defeated	Luke Donald / Pádraig Harrington	3 & 2

All matches completed the following day

True to the weather forecast, Friday dawned ominously. Heavy rain fell over much of the UK. An army of 110 greenkeepers had worked since 5am to clear water from the course.

At 7.45am, with the world watching, Dustin Johnson of the USA hit the first shot of the 38th Ryder Cup. Lee Westwood had requested the honour of commencing for Europe, being the continent's top player, which Colin Montgomerie happily granted. Westwood promptly added the tournament's first birdie at the second hole.

However it became evident over the first few holes that, despite improved drainage and the efforts of the greenkeepers, the ground was saturated.

'Play was suspended at 9.45am due to unplayable conditions.' Announcement by the organisers at 10am Friday morning.

Seven hours and eighteen minutes of play were lost on that first day. The captains, players and caddies retired to the hotel. Spectators walked stoically around the course, keeping warm and dry as best they could, and investigated the eating places, bars and shops.

'... 36.6mm of rain fell between approximately 5.30pm on Thursday and 3.30pm today ... more than 40 percent of the average monthly rainfall fell in less than 24 hours.' Statement from The Celtic Manor Resort.

In one of the more surreal episodes of the week, the USA team reported that their waterproofs were leaking and bought new sets from the on-site shop of a Scottish manufacturer familiar with the maxim 'there's no such thing as bad weather, only the wrong clothes'!

There was a brief resumption of play from 5pm onwards, during which the USA overturned Europe's morning lead. An impressive red sunset helped improve spirits as people looked forward to the following day's resumption of play.

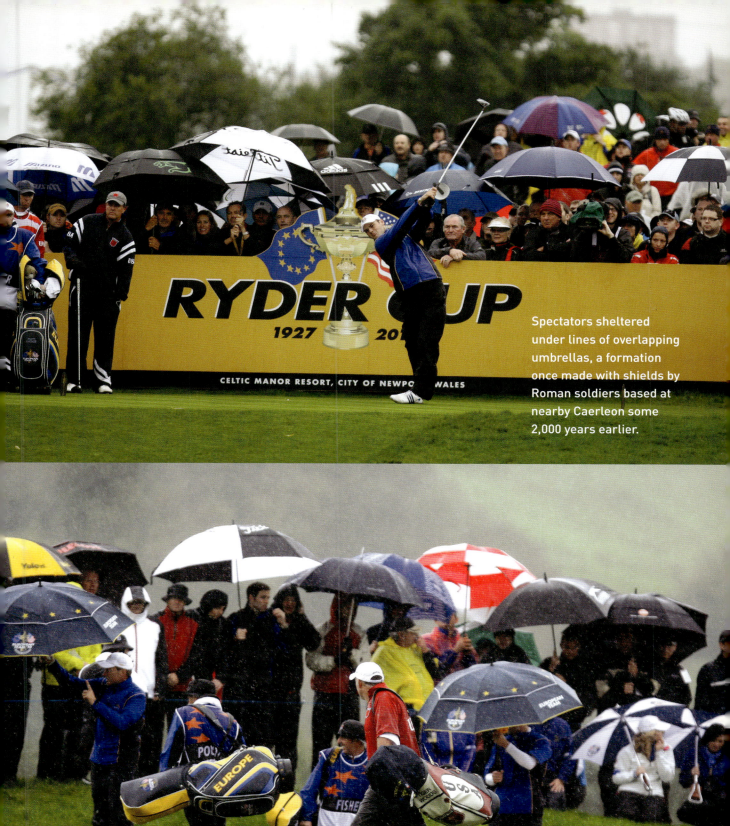

RYDER CUP
1927 – 20[1]
CELTIC MANOR RESORT, CITY OF NEWPORT, WALES

Spectators sheltered under lines of overlapping umbrellas, a formation once made with shields by Roman soldiers based at nearby Caerleon some 2,000 years earlier.

My Ryder Cup The longest weekend

'I feel sorry, really sorry, for the fans out there that have come in their tens of thousands to watch this Ryder Cup, and have met with awful weather conditions.'

Colin Montgomerie

BBC Wales weather presenter Behnaz Akhgar, and the event's own behind-the-scenes forecasters, played a valuable role in enabling organisers – and photographers – to plan ahead.

Despite the weather, European supporters were much encouraged by the amount of blue on the scoreboard on the first morning – though the USA, and especially Stewart Cink, found their putting form and went ahead during the second session.

RYDER C

1927 20

OT 1	RESULT		SUMMARY		DAY 1 FOURBALLS		RESULT	DAY 1 FOU

SUMMARY

DAY 1 FOURBALLS

EUROPE	USA

MATCHES ON THE COURSE

LEAD IN   ALL SQUARE IN   LEAD IN

3		1

PLAY SUSPENDED

RE-START AT

DAY 1 FOURBALLS

			RESULT		
1 07:45	5	WESTWOOD L / KAYMER M	2UP	1 13:15	
		MICKELSON P / JOHNSON D			
2 08:00	4	McILROY R / McDOWELL G	1UP	2 13:30	
		CINK S / KUCHAR M			
3 08:15	3	POULTER I / FISHER R	1UP	3 13:45	
		STRICKER S / WOODS T			
				4 14:00	

The experience of Phil Mickelson and the power of Dustin, his Ryder Cup rookie partner, were kept in check by Lee Westwood and Martin Kaymer.

RYDER CUP

1927 2010

CELTIC MANOR RESORT, CITY OF NEWPORT, WALES

Colin Montgomerie monitored the conditions thoughout the long day, while his team waited patiently. The greenkeepers worked ceaselessly and eventually, as a glimmer of sunshine broke through, the players returned.

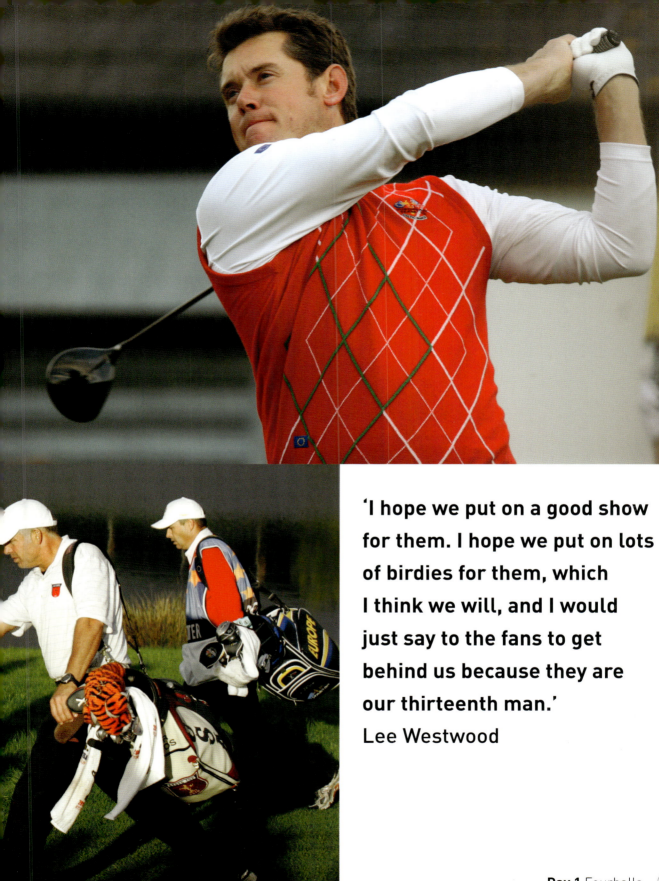

'I hope we put on a good show for them. I hope we put on lots of birdies for them, which I think we will, and I would just say to the fans to get behind us because they are our thirteenth man.'
Lee Westwood

The European players acknowledge the patient crowd at the sixth green.

'They lifted our spirits and were loud and were great. We were able to feed off them.'
Graeme McDowell

It was early days of course, but Stewart Cink was applying all his skill and judgement in his effort to help reverse the European lead.

EUROPE 1 UP
USA

RYDER CUP

'The first tee was a fantastic experience. It was the best atmosphere on a golf course that I have ever felt.'

Rory McIlroy – at 21, Europe's youngest player

Tiger Woods and Ross Fisher experience the close proximity of the spectators. Their cheering and encouragement raised everyone's spirits but once the players stepped up to the tee you could have heard a pin drop.

Tiger Woods put in some
steady work alongside
partner Steve Stricker,
though the towering
form that made him
world No.1 was not yet
in evidence.

'I was there on the 10th green with him, and to hole that putt, you know, it was dark, it was very, very dark. What a roar went up when that putt went in of Poulter's. It must have been, what, 25 feet I suppose, a fantastic effort. That will give us the momentum we need to carry forward into a very, very busy day tomorrow.'
Colin Montgomerie on Ian Poulter's morale-boosting final putt of the day.

'We are still playing for 28 points. Both captains have agreed that after the four fourball matches, which are playing now, the second session will be extended to six foursomes matches. We anticipate that starting mid-morning tomorrow. The third session will comprise two foursomes and four fourballs. That means that by the time they are completed, sometime on Sunday morning, we will have played for 16 points, eight of which are foursomes, eight of which are fourballs. Then we'll have time to schedule the singles on Sunday afternoon and finish on schedule. This all depends on the sky and whether the rain comes back again. We don't have a good forecast for Sunday – if that happens, we will roll into Monday, keeping the singles sacrosanct. Our cut-off point is 6.43pm Monday evening – sunset – and if we are not finished by then, I believe that any match unfinished on the golf course will be considered a halve.'

George O'Grady, Chief Executive of The European Tour, explaining the plan for catching up with the schedule.

Merchandise   Merchandise

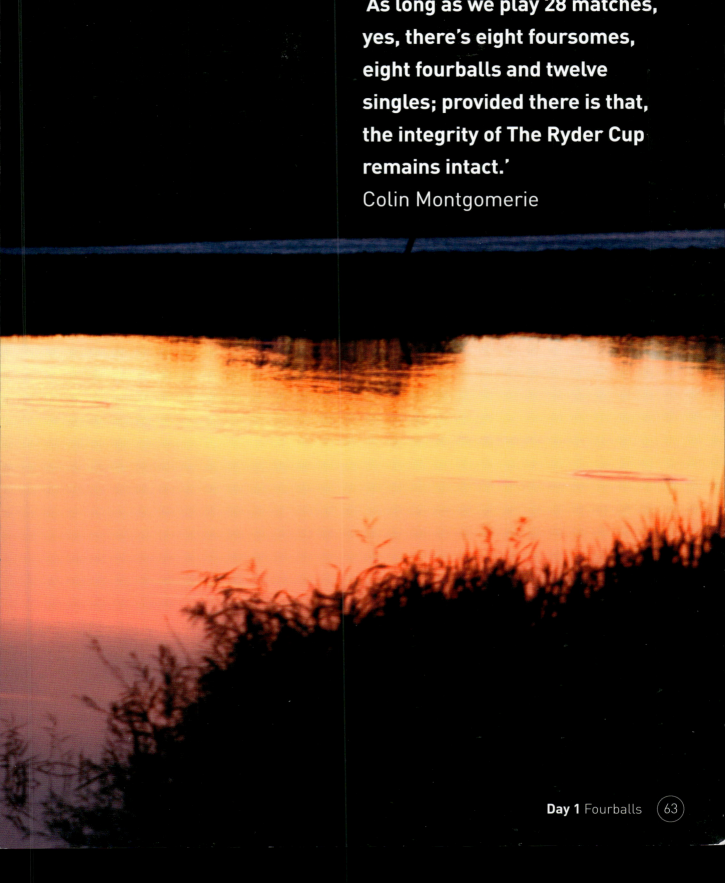

'As long as we play 28 matches, yes, there's eight foursomes, eight fourballs and twelve singles; provided there is that, the integrity of The Ryder Cup remains intact.'
Colin Montgomerie

Day 2
Saturday 2nd October
Foursomes and fourballs

Foursomes

USA		Europe	Score
Tiger Woods / Steve Stricker	Defeated	Miguel Ángel Jiménez / Peter Hanson	4 & 3
Hunter Mahan / Zach Johnson	Defeated	Edoardo Molinari / Francesco Molinari	2 Up
Jim Furyk / Rickie Fowler	Halved	Martin Kaymer / Lee Westwood	Halved
Phil Mickelson / Dustin Johnson	Lost to	Pádraig Harrington / Ross Fisher	3 & 2
Jeff Overton / Bubba Watson	Lost to	Luke Donald / Ian Poulter	2 & 1
Matt Kuchar / Stewart Cink	Defeated	Rory McIlroy / Graeme McDowell	2 Up

A long day lay ahead that would test the stamina of players, caddies, officials and spectators. Six matches, with all 24 players due out on the course, would entertain those fortunate to be there, along with vast television and radio audiences around the world.

The forecast was good and the weather did indeed co-operate, with warm sunshine transforming the course and the surrounding countryside into a very pleasant place to be, as well as drying out the fairways and greens.

The USA endeavoured to consolidate their advantage from the previous evening but Europe put in some fine perfomances and began to generate momentum. The day progressed enjoyably, with exciting matches being completed in quick succession.

Colin Montgomerie had asked for the large screens around the course to show the score more often – between sequences of golfing action – in the expectation that the sight of a lot of European blue would fire up the players and supporters even more. On went the play, with large crowds of fans following their favourites from hole to hole.

'There's going to be a few tired legs tonight, that's for sure.' Lee Westwood

The pace was relentless but the eventual onset of darkness meant that, once again, matches would have to be completed the following day. The USA were in the lead overall but Europe were ahead out on the course. To Colin Montgomerie's cautious satisfaction, the scoreboard was displaying an encouraging mass of blue!

CROESO - WELCOME TO THE 2010 RYDER CUP

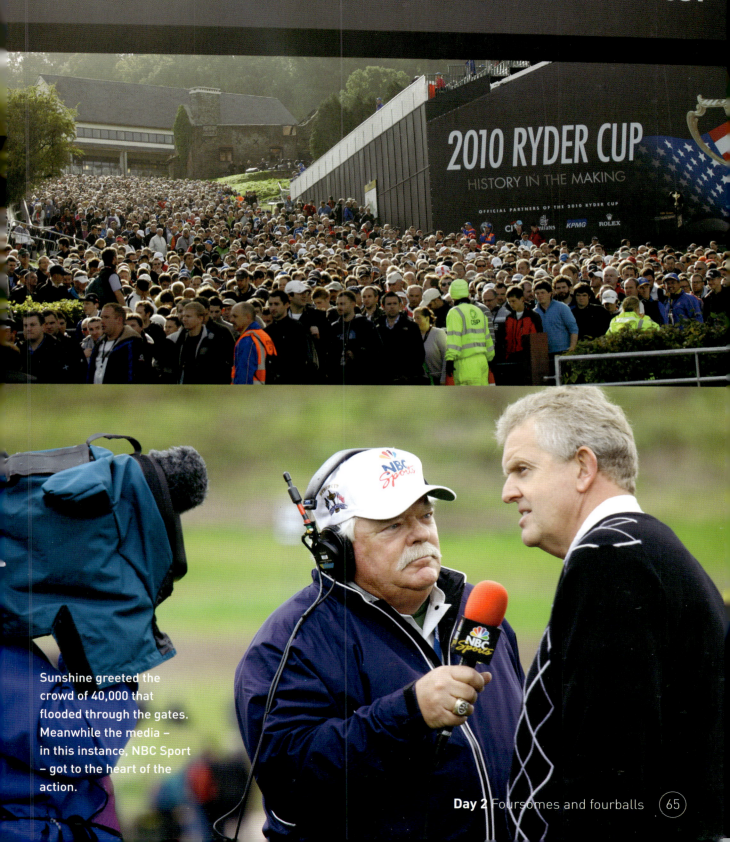

Sunshine greeted the crowd of 40,000 that flooded through the gates. Meanwhile the media – in this instance, NBC Sport – got to the heart of the action.

Ever-reliable Miguel Ángel Jiménez – senior member of the European team – provided his usual vintage blend of steady play and entertainment for the crowd.

KPMG

KPMG

KPMG

E 2010 ER CUP

Tiger Woods and partner Steve Stricker were achieving great consistency, winning every encounter so far:

'We are comfortable with one another and I think that's the biggest thing. Our games complement each other nicely.'
Stricker on Woods

'Stricks played great today, and played great yesterday as well. Any time he was out of the hole, I was in it. We ham-and-egged it pretty well.'
Woods on Stricker

'I think obviously they pair well together and they like it. I was planning on playing them in the first two matches anyway and seeing how it went – and it went well, so they might as well keep going.'
Corey Pavin

Stricker, Woods, Jiménez and Hanson stride down the fairway, Tiger snacking as he goes.

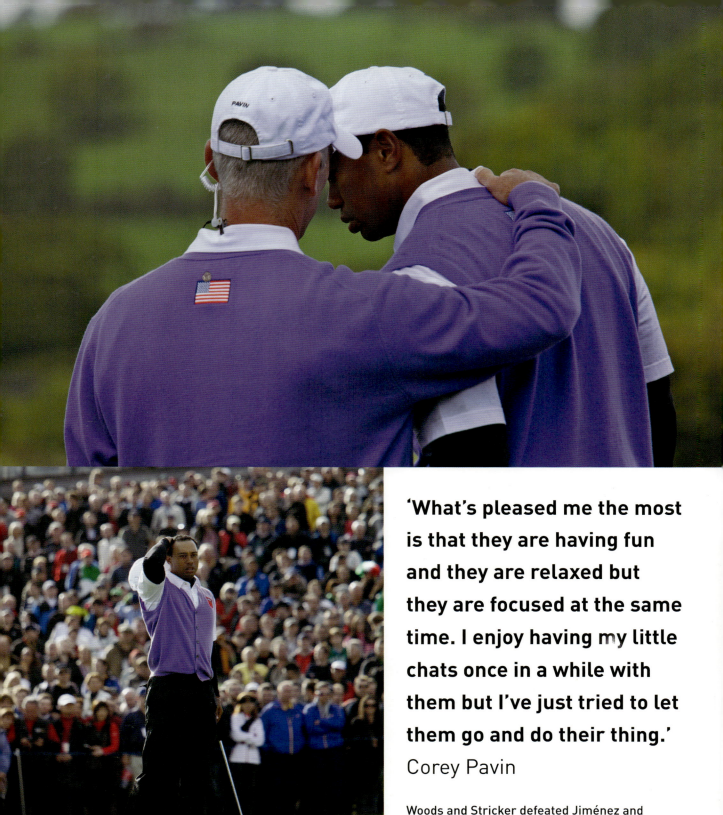

'What's pleased me the most is that they are having fun and they are relaxed but they are focused at the same time. I enjoy having my little chats once in a while with them but I've just tried to let them go and do their thing.'

Corey Pavin

Woods and Stricker defeated Jiménez and Hanson, and also Poulter and Fisher, during this intensive day of golf. Tiger had certainly not forgotten how to roar!

My Ryder Cup The longest weekend

Edoardo and Francesco Molinari became the first brothers to be paired together in The Ryder Cup since Charles and Ernest Whitcombe in 1935.

The players' wives and girlfriends put in a hugely supportive effort, walking miles around the course, often in colourful designer Wellingtons. Corey Pavin paid tribute to them during the closing ceremony, saying: 'They are part of our team!'

'It's quite big news, two brothers in The Ryder Cup. So it's going to be good for golf in Italy.'

Francesco Molinari

'We get along very well with each other since we started to play golf when we were ten or eleven years old, but obviously there was a little bit of competition and rivalry between us. But I think it's been very good for us, because when you see your brother playing better, you want to improve and you want to catch him. I think that's one of the reasons why we're here this week, both of us.'

Edoardo Molinari

Lee Westwood (above)
and Martin Kaymer (below)

My Ryder Cup The longest weekend

'Quite simply, Lee Westwood is my top-ranked player and has proved it. Simple as that. He's been unbelievable; in the team room, in the locker room, on the range, on the course.'

Colin Montgomerie

'Oh, it's so much fun. When the spectators freak out, they stand next to you, screaming at you – it's one of the best days I have ever had on a golf course.'

Martin Kaymer

Ian Poulter and
Luke Donald defeated
Jeff Overton and
Bubba Watson in their
foursomes match,
preserving Luke
Donald's 100 percent
record in Ryder Cup
foursomes, having
played and won five.

In his trademark oversized cap, Rickie Fowler – the youngest member of the USA team, who is just a few weeks older than Rory McIlroy – made a fine impression on his first appearance in the Ryder Cup.

'We could see the scoreboard every few holes. We are obviously keeping an eye on how the other guys are doing and we are trying our best to get our match back to square or possibly be up.'

Rickie Fowler

'It's awesome. Forty thousand fans on home soil. They are always going to give you a buzz, and that's what they did from the first tee onwards. They are priceless.'

Ian Poulter

Tributaries of fans converged and formed a larger – and louder – crowd as play reached the homeward stretch. The broad hillsides provide superb viewing positions overlooking the action.

'It was a really special match out there and, playing against the two Macs, it was really a great two days of match play, today and yesterday. It was really awesome!'
Stewart Cink

'It's amazing, the passion and intensity and the numbers of people that come out. It's really important to be a part of; it is more than I was expecting!'
Matt Kuchar

Graeme McDowell in the bunker below the eighteenth green.

My Ryder Cup The longest weekend

'The team is certainly good enough to survive this. Not down and out by any stretch of the imagination. We still have eighteen points to play for, so – game on!'
Graeme McDowell

'What I want to have out there is those six blue numbers on that left-hand side of that board shining very bright tomorrow morning, and to continue that way. I'm just telling them all how good they are – that's all I can do.'
Colin Montgomerie

Day 3
Sunday 3rd October
Foursomes and fourballs

Foursomes

USA		Europe	Score
Steve Stricker / Tiger Woods	Lost to	Luke Donald / Lee Westwood	6 & 5
Zach Johnson / Hunter Mahan	Lost to	Graeme McDowell / Rory McIlroy	3 & 1

Fourballs

USA		Europe	Score
Dustin Johnson / Jim Furyk	Lost to	Pádraig Harrington / Ross Fisher	2 & 1
Bubba Watson / Jeff Overton	Lost to	Miguel Ángel Jiménez / Peter Hanson	2 Up
Matt Kuchar / Stewart Cink	Halved	Francesco Molinari / Edoardo Molinari	Halved
Phil Mickelson / Rickie Fowler	Lost to	Ian Poulter / Martin Kaymer	2 & 1

Following Europe's return to form the previous evening, the pattern of alternating days of good and bad weather continued to assert itself. Once again, heavy rain fell throughout the night, with the inevitable result.

'Due to severe adverse weather conditions at The Celtic Manor Resort, the organisers of The Ryder Cup have deemed the course currently unplayable. Spectators are advised to remain at home and await further information. Those already at the park-and-ride venues, or currently travelling to the event, are advised to remain in their vehicles.'
Statement by the organisers at 7.30am

Jim McKenzie, Director of Golf Courses at Celtic Manor, was already in action with his eager army of greenkeepers, many of them volunteers. They included the likes of Patrick McAteer, the Course Manager from Nefyn and District Golf Club in north-west Wales – a spectacular clifftop course where they occasionally have to deal with seawater after winter storms. He was typical of the calibre of additional staff from around the UK – and from as far as Ireland, the Netherlands, Scandinavia, Switzerland, Spain and the USA – who worked long and hard to save the event.

Play resumed during the afternoon and brought some thrilling moments. Europe consolidated their advantage and made substantial progress towards their goal of regaining The Ryder Cup. For the first time ever, play would have to continue into an extra day.

Spectators look on with apprehension as rain sweeps into the Usk Valley.

'An additional 15.4mm of rain on Saturday night and Sunday morning meant that a total of 52.2mm (2.04 inches) of rain fell on The Twenty Ten Course between 5.30pm on Thursday and 10am on Sunday. The average monthly rainfall, calculated on the months of September and October, is 94mm (3.7 inches) so the equivalent of 55.5 percent of the average monthly rainfall has fallen in less than three days.'
Statement by The Celtic Manor Resort

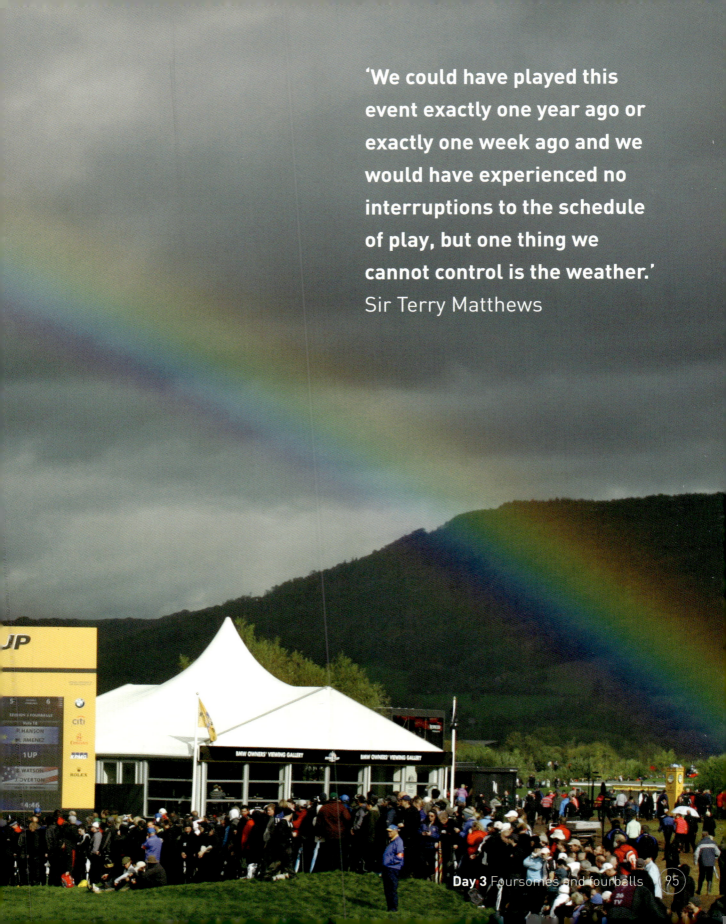

'We could have played this event exactly one year ago or exactly one week ago and we would have experienced no interruptions to the schedule of play, but one thing we cannot control is the weather.'
Sir Terry Matthews

My Ryder Cup The longest weekend

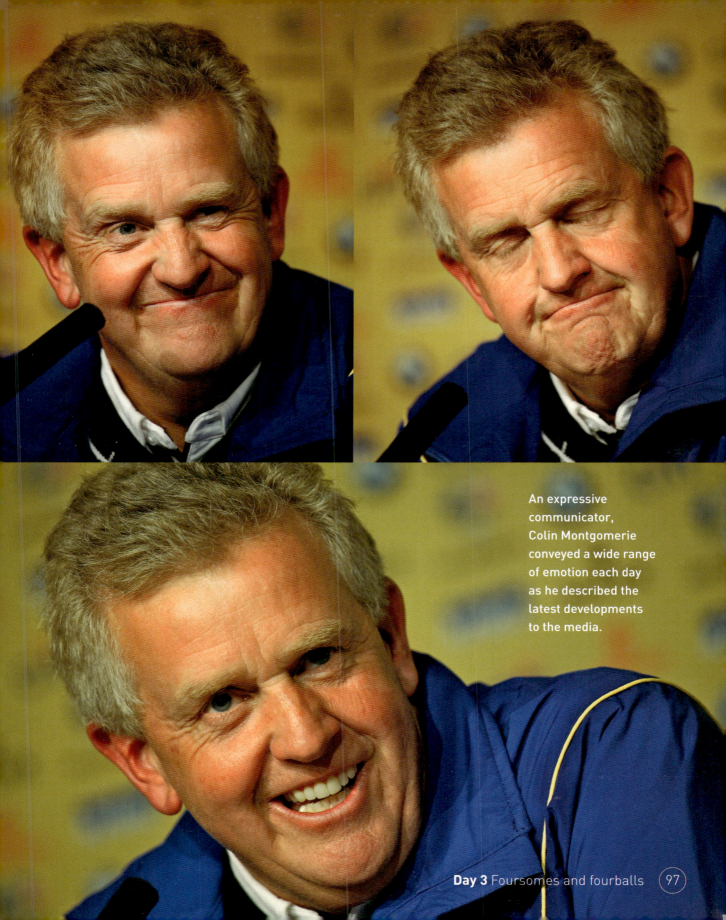

An expressive communicator, Colin Montgomerie conveyed a wide range of emotion each day as he described the latest developments to the media.

Team USA would be three points down by the close of play, with a mountain to climb in the singles the following day, but their fans remained just as enthusiastic as Europe's.

'It was our job to come out stronger than them, and as soon as Lee Westwood holed his first putt from 40 feet down the hill on the tenth, I knew that what we had said last night in the team room remained true; that is, the Americans were going to come out fast and we had to come out faster.'
Colin Montgomerie

'With Lee holing that big putt on 10, you know, it just kind of shut the door; any hope they had became very distant after that.' Luke Donald who, with Lee Westwood, defeated Tiger Woods and Steve Stricker in some style and is seen here accepting a congratulatory handshake from the world No.1.

'Spectators with tickets for Sunday October 3 will be admitted to The Celtic Manor Resort on Monday, October 4, when the final series of singles for The 2010 Ryder Cup is scheduled to start at 9.05am.' Announcement by the organisers.

'I hope that a lot of people take a sickie tomorrow and come out and support the European Team because we know it will do us a lot of good!'

Lee Westwood

Lee Westwood and Luke Donald claimed the biggest foursome victory since 1995. Lee Westwood increased his unbeaten Ryder Cup foursome record to nine matches. Luke Donald extended his 100 percent record to six. Westwood has met Tiger Woods seven times in Ryder Cup matches since 1997 and won six. This was Tiger's heaviest match-play defeat.

EUR	**5**	**OVERALL STANDINGS**	**6**	**USA**	

6 & 5	DONALD WESTWOOD	**F**	STRICKER WOODS	
3 UP	McDOWELL McILROY	**12**	Z. JOHNSON MAHAN	
1 UP	HARRINGTON FISHER	**10**	FURYK D. JOHNSON	
1 UP	HANSON JIMENEZ	**10**	WATSON OVERTON	
1 UP	E. MOLINARI F. MOLINARI	**8**	CINK KUCHAR	
3 UP	POULTER KAYMER	**8**	MICKELSON FOWLER	

As more players finished their matches, the extent of Europe's dominance became clear.

RYDER CUP

EUROPE 3 UP

USA

The challenging holes and marvellous viewing positions – along with the warm welcome and the efficiency of the staff and volunteers – charmed both the players and spectators alike. Everyone was having a great time!

RYDER CUP

THE SINGLES MATCHES TOMORROW.

'Being with Paddy again, you know you're with a great champion – a three-time major champion – and he showed his class. I got him to read my putts and every time I was standing over a putt, I felt so confident knowing that he's reading my putts, and I just hit it on the line he gave me.'

Ross Fisher on Pádraig Harrington

It wasn't over yet. Some in the European camp were sounding a note of caution, recalling the 1999 Ryder Cup at Brookline, USA, when a larger European lead than this was lost.

'That halve point we got in the afternoon, I hope that matters. You know, it's going to be an important first four or five matches tomorrow. They are all going to be important because, you know, if the first four guys go out and win, then that puts the importance on that last halve.'

Stewart Cink

'We have got twelve of the best players in the world – twelve of the best players! Europe have twelve of the best players in the world, too. Match play – anything can happen!'

Corey Pavin

With players spread
out over the long and
convoluted course, the
cheers and chants of the
fans played an important
role in boosting
motivation on the
remoter stretches, often
indicating success by
team mates elsewhere.

As shadows lengthened the entertainment continued. Ian Poulter extricated himself well from a bunker guarding the sixteenth green as he and Martin Kaymer overwhelmed Phil Mickelson and Rickie Fowler.

Day 4
Monday 4th October
Singles

USA		Europe	Score
Steve Stricker	Defeated	Lee Westwood	2 & 1
Stewart Cink	Halved	Rory McIlroy	Halved
Jim Furyk	Lost to	Luke Donald	1 Up
Dustin Johnson	Defeated	Martin Kaymer	6 & 4
Matt Kuchar	Lost to	Ian Poulter	5 & 4
Jeff Overton	Defeated	Ross Fisher	3 & 2
Bubba Watson	Lost to	Miguel Ángel Jiménez	4 & 3
Tiger Woods	Defeated	Francesco Molinari	4 & 3
Rickie Fowler	Halved	Edoardo Molinari	Halved
Phil Mickelson	Defeated	Peter Hanson	4 & 2
Zach Johnson	Defeated	Pádraig Harrington	3 & 2
Hunter Mahan	Lost to	Graeme McDowell	3 & 1

Monday morning brought wide grins to the faces of the organisers as 35,000 people loyally filed in to The Celtic Manor Resort. Many a tolerant employer must have turned a blind eye that day! It was just as well that entry had not been extended beyond those who held Sunday's tickets; the likely overcrowding would surely have been a safety nightmare.

What a day of golf lay ahead! The USA were in storming form and whittled away at Europe's lead. As the afternoon drew on, the Americans clawed their way towards a cliffhanger finish, placing the weight of success or failure on the shoulders of Graeme McDowell and Hunter Mahan in the last singles match. McDowell – the reigning Wales Open and US Open champion – rose confidently to the challenge and, in a gripping finish, sealed the memorable team victory that would bring The Ryder Cup back to Europe.

It had been a rollercoaster ride. The physical demands caused by the atrocious weather had tested everyone's stamina and good humour. But then, if there hadn't been such adversity there wouldn't have been a need for such a glorious response by all concerned.

Fog covered the course early that morning. The singing and banter of the European fans attained new peaks of witty inventiveness. 'Where's the fairway gone?' to the tune of 'Where's your mama gone?' was their early contribution to the day's entertainment.

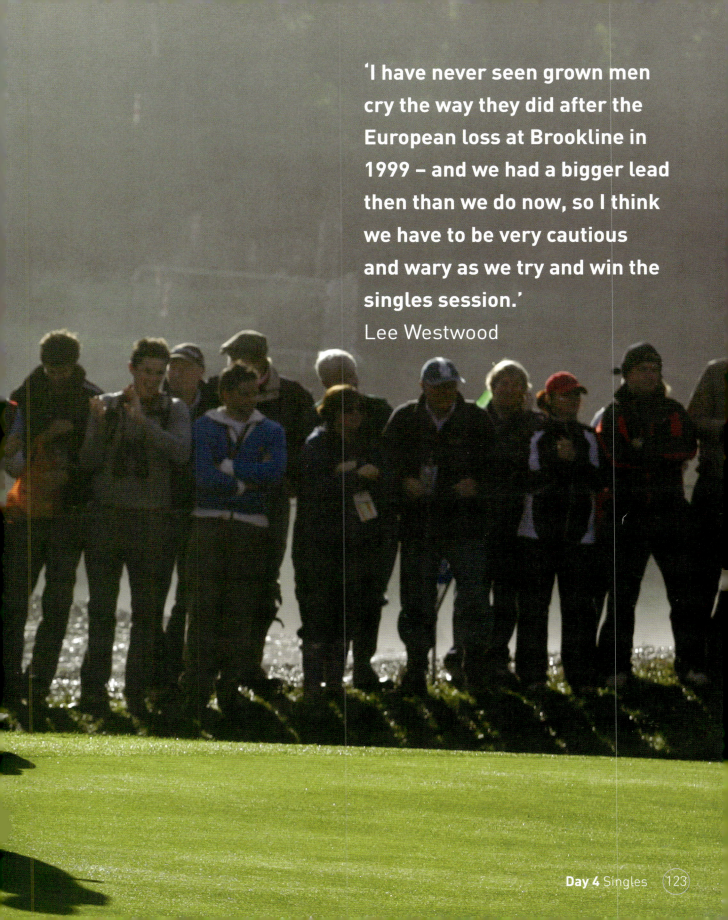

'I have never seen grown men cry the way they did after the European loss at Brookline in 1999 – and we had a bigger lead then than we do now, so I think we have to be very cautious and wary as we try and win the singles session.'

Lee Westwood

'Lend us a tenner Jim!'

European fans to Jim Furyk, who had won over $11 million in the FedEx Cup in the USA the week before. He sportingly made a show of looking for his wallet! Rickie Fowler, unfamiliar with his namesake in the BBC soap opera East Enders, was perplexed by shouts of **'Where's Bianca?'**

Wales
Cymru

The course basked in pleasant morning sunshine and the fog quickly cleared. Team USA got on with putting in the work that would bring them close – so close – to victory.

The Twenty Ten Course is second-to-none in its combination of challenging features, excellent spectator access and pleasing location. For much of the year the weather co-operates, enabling members and visitors to enjoy tremendous golf – as The Ryder Cup teams were also able to do in Monday's sunshine.

'**We've got G-Mac, you've got Big Mac.**' European fans' singing in tribute to Graeme McDowell.

'**Does that make me Wee Mac?**' Rory McIlroy's response after hearing the above.

'To win this, to regain The Ryder Cup and bring it back to European soil – to do it for European golf and for Seve and for everyone involved – it's been the best week of my life. In two years' time, I do not want to be watching this on television!' Rory McIlroy, who escaped from the bunker on the eighteenth at his second attempt, while halving with Stewart Cink.

Ian Poulter, unshakeably confident throughout the week, was clearly pleased with his contribution to the score, having beaten Matt Kuchar.

As play ebbed and flowed, Ross Fisher gave good account of himself but was defeated by Jeff Overton.

'I like it here – not only this golf course, but the other golf courses – and I come here every year to play. I like the place and I like the people and I feel good here.'
Miguel Ángel Jiménez, describing The Celtic Manor Resort.

'Fantastico! Beautiful!'
Miguel Ángel Jiménez, giving his opinion of the European supporters.

'Well, I played well today, and it was nice to turn my match around. I've been close to playing that way for a little bit now, but really looking forward to the rest of the year – I have three more events.'
Tiger Woods, reflecting on the week in which he seemed to regain full form following a time of turbulence in his personal life.

EUR	12	OVERALL STANDINGS	9	USA	
L. WESTWOOD	F			S. STRICKER	2&1
R. MCILROY	F			S. CINK	AS
L. DONALD	F			J. FURYK	
M. KAYMER	F			D. JOHNSON	6&4
I. POULTER	F			M. KUCHAR	
R. FISHER	14			J. OVERTON	2UP
M. JIMENEZ	14			B. WATSON	
F. MOLINARI	13			T. WOODS	4UP
E. MOLINARI	13			R. FOWLER	
P. HANSON	12			P. MICKELSON	3UP
P. HARRINGTON	11			Z. JOHNSON	4UP
G. MCDOWELL	11			H. MAHAN	

THE 2010 RYDER CUP

rydercup

Francesco Molinari went down to a resurgent Tiger Woods and Edoardo halved with a sparklingly on-form Rickie Fowler.

The brothers had won the hearts of the supporters and made an honourable contribution to Europe's total score.

Edoardo Molinari playing
out of the sand trap
against Ricky Fowler.

'Rickie was amazing – he birdied fifteen, sixteen, seventeen and eighteen. His putt on eighteen was incredible. From a twenty-one year old, it was amazing. He's that kind of kid and I think we'll see him a lot more in The Ryder Cup in the future.'

Corey Pavin on Rickie Fowler's distinguished performance.

Peter Hanson lining up
a tricky putt against
Phil Mickelson.

'We appreciate the way the
people here in Wales have
treated us, because they've
been very supportive of the
European team and very
respectful towards us, and we
thank them.' Phil Mickelson,
who defeated Peter Hanson.

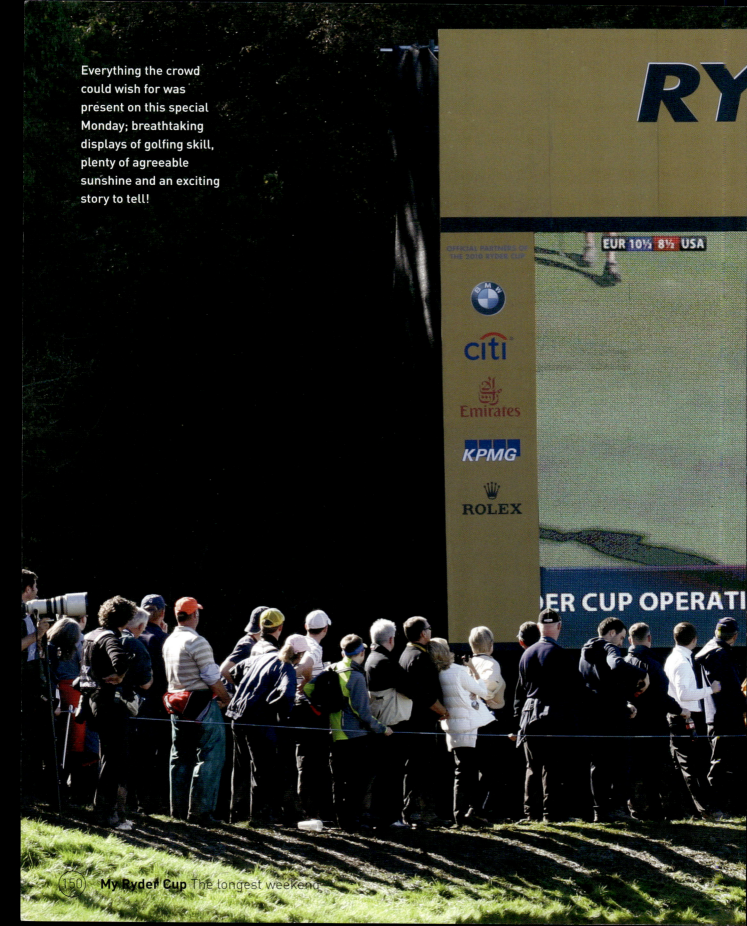

Everything the crowd
could wish for was
present on this special
Monday; breathtaking
displays of golfing skill,
plenty of agreeable
sunshine and an exciting
story to tell!

EUR 10½ 8½ USA

OFFICIAL PARTNERS OF
THE 2010 RYDER CUP

RY

DER CUP OPERATI

RYDER CUP 1927 — 2010

OFFICE....

	OVERALL STANDINGS	
10½		8½

SINGLES

Hole 11

M. JIMENEZ

3 UP

B. WATSON

Match 7 RUNNING

Hole 10

F. MOLINARI

1 UP

T. WOODS

Match 8 RUNNING

13 9

OFFICIAL PARTNERS OF THE 2010 RYDER CUP

BMW

citi

Emirates

KPMG

ROLEX

Pádraig Harrington was a favourite with the fans and made a valuable contribution as mentor and adviser to some of the new faces in the European team.

'I finished off with guys I thought could handle the pressure of a Ryder Cup win on their shoulders. The last three spots in particular – I felt that Phil, Zach and Hunter were good people to have in the very high-pressure situation that could develop in those slots.' Corey Pavin, explaining his selection; Phil Mickelson and Zach Johnson (pictured here) did indeed meet their captain's expectations, but Hunter Mahan would be less fortunate.

Vales

'What we care about is that these matches were played to completion and they were played fairly, in great sportsmanship. I thought the fans were fantastic all week – they were respectful. I thought that, in all of the matches, the players played with great pride on both sides. And it was a very, very fair fight.'

Corey Pavin

Bon appétit. Or mwynhewch eich bwyd as we like to say.

'Hats off to the fans here. They are obviously cheering their team on, but I felt like we were given new respect. It's a home-field advantage, as it should be, but I think they did it in the proper way.'
Jim Furyk

'It was just a joy. You know, you hear about soccer matches over here, and the people chanting and cheering – to hear it first-hand was pretty exciting. They had some good songs going!'
Bubba Watson

'To hear that kind of excitement for golf really is spectacular for us. We don't get a chance to play in front of crowds that boisterous and spirited!'
Stewart Cink

'Graeme was put last for a good reason; he is full of confidence and that showed. That birdie on sixteen was quite unbelievable, quite unbelievable!'

Colin Montgomerie

As Graeme McDowell took in the significance of the results, he realised that the fate of his team rested squarely with him and his ability to hold off the challenge of Hunter Mahan. He held his nerve, and continued making tremendous shots, especially his perfect putt – under huge pressure – on the sixteenth.

Hunter Mahan ultimately lost his composure and made a couple of uncharacteristic errors on his approach to the seventeenth.

Graeme McDowell was spared any further pressure – it was all over and The Ryder Cup would be staying in Europe.

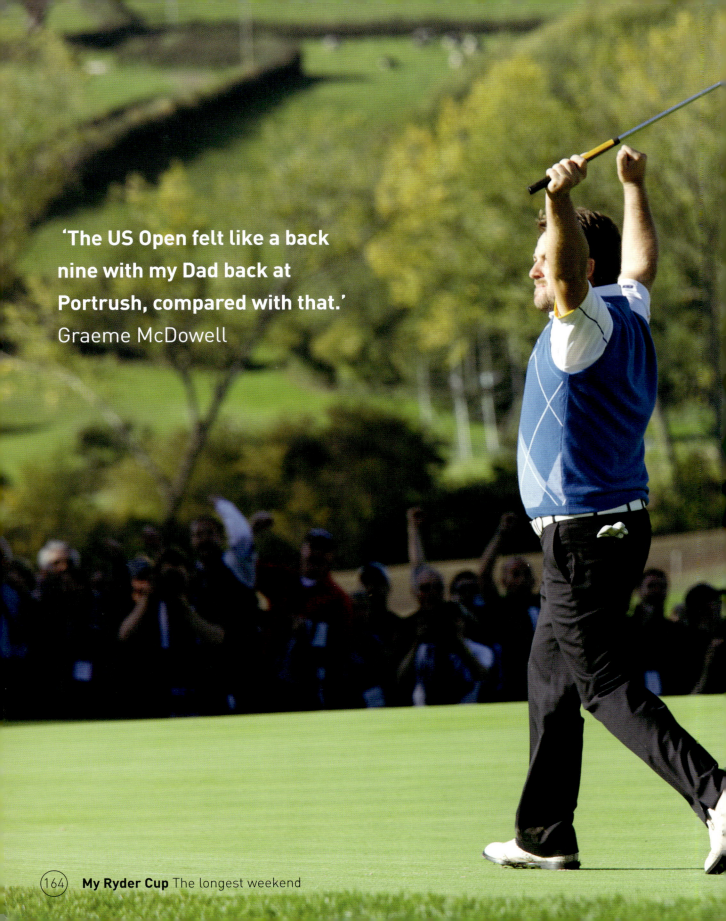

'The US Open felt like a back nine with my Dad back at Portrush, compared with that.'
Graeme McDowell

Europe 14½

USA 13½

Rory McIlroy heads through the fans towards the clubhouse – it is clearly going to take a while!

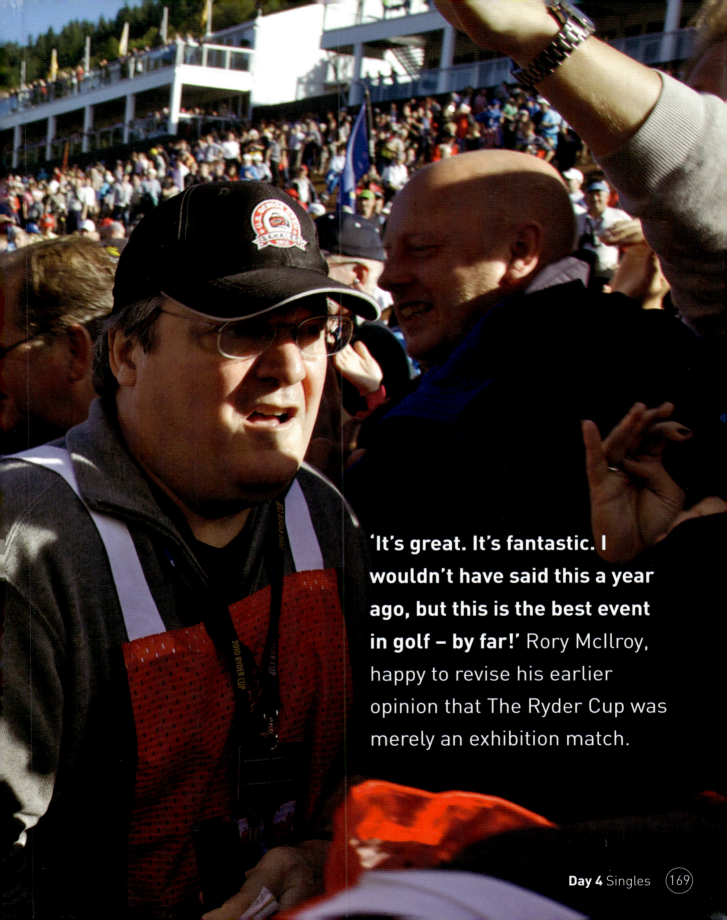

'It's great. It's fantastic. I wouldn't have said this a year ago, but this is the best event in golf – by far!' Rory McIlroy, happy to revise his earlier opinion that The Ryder Cup was merely an exhibition match.

'There's no tournament that I get fired up for more than The Ryder Cup. There's no money on the line. It's just about pride, passion, putting your heart on your sleeve and going out and winning some points and that's why I enjoy it so much.' Luke Donald, second from right, with (left to right) Lee Westwood, Ross Fisher and Peter Hanson.

'I think that this Ryder Cup is definitely the best show on earth as far as golf goes. I love it!' Graeme McDowell, celebrating with Pádraig Harrington.

Closing ceremony

The 2010 Ryder Cup was a huge success. The Celtic Manor Resort proved to be a superlative venue. The Twenty Ten Course secured its place as one of the world's great tests of golfing skill.

The players took a break while supporters savoured the momentous events and bought souvenirs of the historic day on which The Ryder Cup was won back for Europe. There was an upbeat mood and the sun continued to shine.

A large photograph of Severiano Ballesteros – one of the true greats of golf and a former Ryder Cup captain – was carried to the stage, to respectful applause. Battling illness at home in Spain, Seve was unable to be present but a telephone call from him, relayed on speaker-phone in the European team room, had reinforced the determination and unity of the players.

The stage filled for a second time, the teams receiving a rapturous welcome. Thanks were extended to everyone who had made the event a success. The First Minister of Wales presented The Ryder Cup to Colin Montgomerie and invited everyone to come back and visit Wales soon. At the end of a remarkable week, those present reflected on a Ryder Cup that began with a battle against the elements; was able to continue because of a heroic response from staff, volunteers, players and spectators; and will rightly be remembered for having thrilled the world with truly exhilarating golf.

The Wales Open, held on The Twenty Ten Course each summer, will have gained stature by association with The Ryder Cup – and as the springboard for Graeme McDowell's victory in the 2010 US Open. Many people will have been inspired to take up golf for the first time and many youngsters, given coaching as part of an outreach effort in the years leading up to the event, will be earnestly practising in the hope of achieving great things.

Given a few weeks of care and attention from the greenkeepers, the course would recover from the beating it had received. From this day on, The Twenty Ten Course would be spoken of with admiration and wonderment as the venue for one of the greatest golf contests of all time. Yes, for many reasons, The Ryder Cup of 2010 – the longest weekend – was certainly an occasion to remember!

The teams returned to the stage for the closing ceremony. Colin Montgomerie called forward each of the European players in turn to receive the applause of the jubilant fans. Miguel Ángel Jiménez played to the crowd, draped in the Spanish flag.

Carwyn Jones, First
Minister of Wales,
presented The Ryder Cup
to Colin Montgomerie
to thunderous applause
and the loudest cheers
of the week.

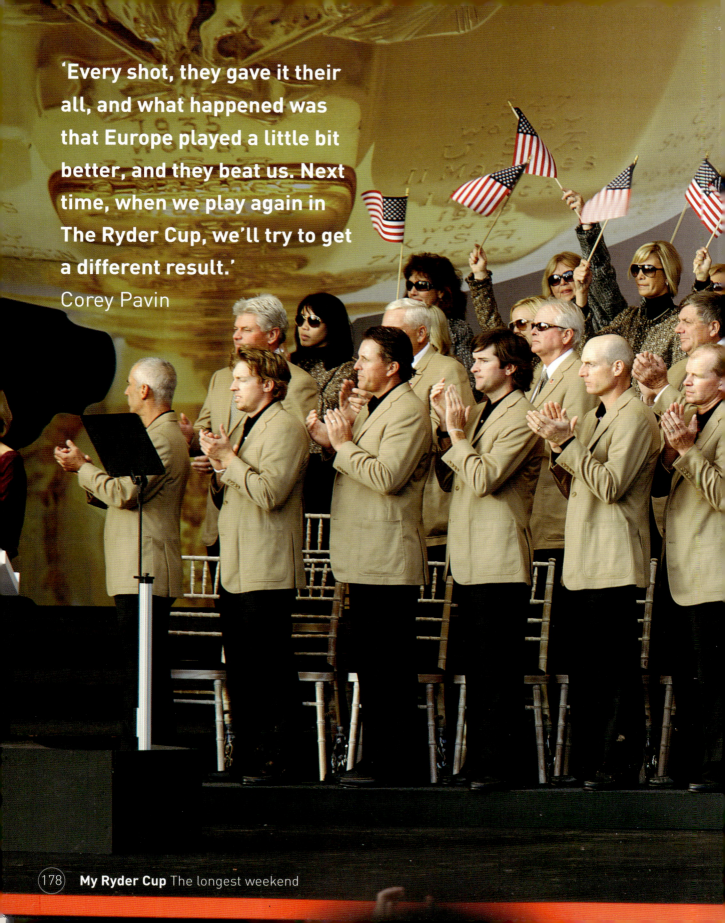

'Every shot, they gave it their all, and what happened was that Europe played a little bit better, and they beat us. Next time, when we play again in The Ryder Cup, we'll try to get a different result.'

Corey Pavin

To crown an amazing day, Lee Westwood was also promoted to No.2 in the world rankings and Martin Kaymer followed within a month to No.3, placing them within reach of the top spot, held by Tiger Woods.

'One ginger Spaniard, there's only one ginger Spaniard, one ginger Spaaaaaniard!' Sung by fans, to the tune of Guantanamera, to the great delight of Miguel Ángel Jiménez. The same tune also served for **'Two Molinaris, there's only two Molinaris.'**

'Sixteen was massive. You know, it was a fast putt – I just had to get it going – and thankfully it caught an edge. Wow! It was the best putt I've ever hit in my life!'

Graeme McDowell

The strong Irish contingent – Pádraig Harrington, Graeme McDowell, Rory McIlroy and vice-captain Darren Clarke – take a moment to celebrate with the trophy.

'I'm very proud. It's a very proud moment for us all here in Europe. They all played, to a man, magnificently – they all gave 110 per cent and that's all you can ask.'

Colin Montgomerie

Colin Montgomerie,
centre, with the victorious
European team.

Back row, left to right:
Luke Donald,
Lee Westwood,
Martin Kaymer,
Peter Hanson,
Pádraig Harrington,
Ross Fisher, Ian Poulter,
Miguel Ángel Jiménez.

Front row, left to right:
Francesco Molinari,
Edoardo Molinari,
Rory McIlroy,
Graeme McDowell.

NOR RESORT CITY OF NEWPOR

WALES 1 - 3 OCTOBER

The elation of the team was evident at the final media conference, as they told the world how they won The Ryder Cup!

Closing ceremony

Match results

Day 1 Friday 1st October – Saturday 2nd October, Fourballs

USA		Europe	Score
Phil Mickelson / Dustin Johnson	Lost to	Lee Westwood / Martin Kaymer	3 & 2 ●
Stewart Cink / Matt Kuchar	Halved	Rory McIlroy / Graeme McDowell	Halved ●●
Tiger Woods / Steve Stricker	Defeated	Ross Fisher / Ian Poulter	2 Up ●
Bubba Watson / Jeff Overton	Defeated	Luke Donald / Pádraig Harrington	3 & 2 ●

Day 2 Saturday 2nd October, Foursomes

USA		Europe	Score
Tiger Woods / Steve Stricker	Defeated	Miguel Ángel Jiménez / Peter Hanson	4 & 3 ●
Hunter Mahan / Zach Johnson	Defeated	Edoardo Molinari / Francesco Molinari	2 Up ●
Jim Furyk / Rickie Fowler	Halved	Martin Kaymer / Lee Westwood	Halved ●●
Phil Mickelson / Dustin Johnson	Lost to	Pádraig Harrington / Ross Fisher	3 & 2 ●
Jeff Overton / Bubba Watson	Lost to	Luke Donald / Ian Poulter	2 & 1 ●
Matt Kuchar / Stewart Cink	Defeated	Rory McIlroy / Graeme McDowell	1 Up ●

Day 3 Sunday 3rd October, Foursomes and Fourballs

USA		Europe	Score
Steve Stricker / Tiger Woods	Lost to	Luke Donald / Lee Westwood	6 & 5 ●
Zach Johnson / Hunter Mahan	Lost to	Graeme McDowell / Rory McIlroy	3 & 1 ●
Dustin Johnson / Jim Furyk	Lost to	Pádraig Harrington / Ross Fisher	2 & 1 ●
Bubba Watson / Jeff Overton	Lost to	Miguel Ángel Jiménez / Peter Hanson	2 Up ●
Matt Kuchar / Stewart Cink	Halved	Francesco Molinari / Edoardo Molinari	Halved ●●
Phil Mickelson / Rickie Fowler	Lost to	Ian Poulter / Martin Kaymer	2 & 1 ●

Day 4 Monday 4th October, Singles

USA		Europe	Score
Steve Stricker	Defeated	Lee Westwood	2 & 1 ●
Stewart Cink	Halved	Rory McIlroy	Halved ●●
Jim Furyk	Lost to	Luke Donald	1 Up ●
Dustin Johnson	Defeated	Martin Kaymer	6 & 4 ●
Matt Kuchar	Lost to	Ian Poulter	5 & 4 ●
Jeff Overton	Defeated	Ross Fisher	3 & 2 ●
Bubba Watson	Lost to	Miguel Ángel Jiménez	4 & 3 ●
Tiger Woods	Defeated	Francesco Molinari	4 & 3 ●
Rickie Fowler	Halved	Edoardo Molinari	Halved ●●
Phil Mickelson	Defeated	Peter Hanson	4 & 2 ●
Zach Johnson	Defeated	Pádraig Harrington	3 & 2 ●
Hunter Mahan	Lost to	Graeme McDowell	3 & 1 ●

Holes won USA ● Europe ●

Holes halved ●●

Europe 14½   USA 13½

The Welsh flag – The Red Dragon – was lowered by a Welsh Guard and The Ryder Cup was brought to a close.

Useful websites
europeantour.com
pgatour.com
rydercup.com
visitwales.co.uk
celtic-manor.com
graffeg.com